The big 5
and other wild animals

Elephant
Megan Emmett

The big 5 and other wild animals series is published by
Awareness Publishing Group (Pty) Ltd.
Copyright © 2019

Awareness Publishing (SA) (Pty) Ltd
www.awareness.co.za
info@awareness.co.za
+27 (0)86 110 1491
www.facebook.com/AwarenessPublishing

All rights reserved. No part of this publication may be reproduced in any form without written permission from the publisher, except by a reviewer.

First edition, 2019

Elephant by Megan Emmett
ISBN 978-0-6393-0010-8

Summary: An introduction to the elephant, one of the Big Five wild animals. This book looks at the elephant's physical characteristics, its daily activities, and its family life and home ranges. The book also talks about the conservation of elephants.

Book design: Dana Espag and Bianca Keenan-Smith.

Editorial credits: Educational consultant: Gillian Mervis. Copy editor: Danya Ristić. Proofreader: Lynda Gilfillan. Picture editor: Anne Laing. Indexer: Lois C Henderson.

Illustrations: Cartoons: Gerhard Cruywagen of Greenhouse Cartoons, and Dana Espag. Additional drawings: Dana Espag.

Photo credits: Cover and pp.3 (top and middle), 4, 6, 8, 9, 10, 11 (top), 13, 15, 16, 17 (left and right), 22, 24, 25 (left and right), 26, 27 (left and right), 28, 30, 31, 33, 34, 36 (bottom left), 38, 44 (top and bottom), 46, 48, 49, 52, and 56 © Anne Laing; pp.3 (bottom), 11 (bottom), 12 (top left and right, bottom right), 36 (top left), 40, 42, 60 and 66 © Shem Compion; pp.12 (bottom left), 14, 22 (inset), 29 (top), 32, 41, 59 and 61 © Megan Emmett; p.17 (middle) © DaveThomasNZ; p.18 © Alamy Images / AfriPics; p.20 © dkmurphypr / flickr; p.29 (bottom) © Cameron Spencer / iStockphoto; p.36 (top right) © Sean Nel / Shutterstock; (bottom right) © Leopardinatree / iStockphoto; p.39 © Alamy Images / AfriPics; p.50 © P de Graaf / Gallo Images; p.51 © Alamy Images / AfriPics; p.54 © Debbie Aird Photography / Shutterstock; p.58 © Fred Bruemmer / Gallo Images; p.62 © Alamy Images / AfriPics; p.64 © AfriPics.

You can read more by Megan Emmett about animals in the book *Game Ranger in Your Backpack – All-in-one Interpretative Guide to the Lowveld*, published by Briza Publications (2010, Pretoria). ISBN 978-1-920217-06-8.

1 3 5 7 9 0 8 6 4 2

Contents

Quick facts 7
Meet the elephant 9
Great big ears 11
Useful trunk 13
What are tusks for? 15
More uses for tusks 17
Big teeth 19
How the teeth get replaced 21
Elephant graveyards 23
Male and female elephants 25
Senses 27
Big feet 29
Walking quietly 31
Rumbles 33
Water 35
Swimming 37
Mud! 39
Family life 41
Young bulls and old bulls 43
Clans and home ranges 45
Social life 47
Musth 49

Some older female elephants, like the one on the left, have large, thick tusks.

Contents continued

Finding a mate..51
Food 53
Habits..55
When danger comes..57
Helping the bush 59
Elephants and people 61
Conservation..63
Culling 65
Glossary..67

Words that appear in the text in bold, **like this**, are explained in the Glossary at the end of this book. Some key words are in colour.

A male elephant can weigh up to six tons!

Quick facts

Height (at the shoulder)	Male: three metres Female: 2,5 metres
Weight	Male: Up to six tons; the heaviest bull ever weighed was 6,6 tons. Female: Up to four tons
Lifespan	55–60 years
Gestation (pregnancy)	22 months
Number of young	One at a time
Habitat	Anywhere in Africa that has enough food to eat, shade to rest in and water to drink – this could be swamps, forests, woodland, bushveld, grassland, hills and mountains, and even deserts
Food	Plants, including grass, herbs, water plants, bulbs, tubers, roots, fruits, flowers, tree bark, wood, pods, seeds, leaves and branches
Predators	Young elephants are eaten by lions and hyena. In some areas adults are killed by lions
Is it one of the Big Five?	Yes!

The elephant on the right is helping the mother on the left to make shade for her hot, exhausted baby.

Meet the elephant

The African elephant is the largest and heaviest land animal in the world. Elephants have huge grey bodies with big ears. And they have a long trunk instead of a nose. Elephants are powerful but gentle animals.

Elephants eat whatever food that they can find. In times of drought, when there has been little or no rain, there may be no food. At these times, elephants may move to new areas to find food, covering large distances.

Elephants are extremely clever animals. They can remember things for a long time. They also care about other elephants in their family, and they help sick or hurt members of the herd.

Because elephants are so powerful, they can be dangerous. They are part of a group that we call the Big Five. The Big Five are the largest and most dangerous animals in the wild. The other animals in this group are buffalo, rhino, lion and leopard. Long ago, people from Europe used to come to Africa to hunt the Big Five, especially elephants, to prove and show how brave they were. Nowadays, many people go on holiday to a game reserve to see the Big Five.

veins

Keeping the body temperature just right

On hot days, elephants spray mud or water behind their ears. This helps to cool the blood in the ears, and the cooler blood flows to the rest of the body. When the weather is cold, elephants hold their ears close to their bodies. This keeps the blood in their veins warm, at the right temperature.

Elephants have many veins close to the surface of the skin behind their ears. These veins help the elephant to keep cool.

Great big ears

Elephants have huge ears. The ear of a male, or bull, elephant weighs up to 20 kilograms and can be more than a metre wide! Elephants use their ears in various ways.

First, their ears are used for listening to sounds. The ears collect and send sounds into the eardrums. The eardrums are inside the ear-holes, which are just in front of the flaps.

Second, elephants use their ears to show what they are feeling. For example, when an elephant flaps its ears, it may be showing that it is angry or annoyed.

Third, an elephant's ears help to keep its body at the right temperature. For example, the ears keep it cool in hot weather. By slowly flapping its ears, the elephant makes a breeze of light wind that flows over its ears. This breeze cools the warm blood in the ears. The surface area of the ears is large – about 20 per cent of an elephant's body – and the skin over the ears is quite thin. There are many veins, or blood vessels, in this skin, and an elephant pumps all of its blood through its ears every 20 minutes. So about 12 litres of blood passes through its ears every minute. The cool blood then flows from the ears to the rest of the elephant's body and cools it.

The elephant's eardrum is inside a hole in front of its big ear flap.

An elephant throws sand behind its ears, to create a sun screen and to prevent parasites from living there.

The folds of skin allow the trunk to shrink or stretch so the elephant can reach different foods.

An elephant uses its trunk to suck up water, which it then squirts into its mouth and swallows.

Elephants use the tips of their trunks like two fingers to pick up food and other objects.

Elephants use their trunks to throw sand, mud or water on their bodies.

Useful trunk

The elephant's nose and its top lip make up its long trunk. No other animal has a trunk. The elephant uses its trunk as an arm, a nose, and also as a straw to drink with. The trunk is very sensitive to touch, which means that the elephant easily feels things that its trunk touches.

In the trunk there are thousands of muscles, and these muscles help the elephant to use its trunk in many ways. An elephant stretches its trunk to reach things. And it **shrinks** the trunk to make it easier to carry when it moves around.

The trunk helps the elephant to collect and eat different types of food. The elephant also breathes air through its trunk. It sucks up water with its trunk, often many litres at a time. Once the elephant has sucked up the water, it squirts it into its mouth to swallow it.

Elephants pick fruit off trees with the tips of their trunks. They can grasp and take hold of a single berry, because the end of the trunk is almost like two fingers. Elephants use the side of their trunks to scoop, or pick up, piles of fruit that have fallen onto the ground. The trunk is also strong enough to break big branches off trees, and to tear the leaves off.

Elephants enjoy taking a mud bath. They suck dust or mud from the ground with their trunks. Then they spray the dust or mud over their bodies to keep cool and to protect their skin from insects that may bite it.

Did you know?

Baby elephants cannot use their trunks well until they are three months old. Until then, their trunks just flop around. It takes a lot of time and practice for baby elephants to learn the complex ways of using and controlling their trunks.

Tusks are huge teeth that stick out of the elephant's mouth.

What are tusks for?

Elephants have two long white teeth that stick out on either side of their mouths. These teeth are called tusks. The tusks keep growing through the elephant's life, becoming larger as the elephant gets older.

The tusks end in a point. Elephants use their tusks to protect themselves and their families from **predators** such as lions. Sometimes, elephants fight with one another. The elephants then use their tusks to protect themselves.

Elephants also use their tusks as tools when they are feeding. They use their tusks to clean off any soil that may be on a plant. They use them like spades to dig plants and roots from the ground. They also use their tusks like a lever to pull branches down or to tear bark off trees.

Two young elephants tussle and fight each other using their tusks.

Sometimes an elephant loses a tusk.

More uses for tusks

An elephant's tusks are **unique**. This means that no two elephants have the same tusks. Some elephants have huge tusks, while others, of the same age, may have small tusks or even no tusks at all.

An elephant's tusks can break when the elephant fights with another elephant, or when the elephant uses them to push trees down onto the ground.

Tusks become worn down, or shorter, with use. An elephant usually uses one tusk more than it uses the other, just like we use one hand more than we use the other. The tusk that the elephant uses more often will be the shorter tusk.

Very old bulls do not use their tusks as much as younger bulls do. This is because they are too old to mate and they no longer fight other males to win females. Their tusks can become very big and long, because they no longer get worn down.

The largest tusk ever found in the Kruger National Park weighed 64 kilograms! And the longest tusk ever measured was 3,55 metres long!

One molar tooth

An elephant with its mouth open, showing its two upper molar teeth.

Big teeth

Each tooth inside an elephant's mouth is large, so large that it can be the size of a brick and can weigh over four kilograms in a fully grown elephant! The teeth are flat with hard lines, or ridges, across them. These teeth are called molars.

In its lifetime, an elephant grows six sets of teeth, each of four molars. There is always one molar on each side of each jaw: one molar in the upper left jaw, a second in the upper right jaw, a third in the lower left jaw, and a fourth in the lower right jaw. As the elephant grows from a baby to an adult, one set of four teeth is replaced by a new set of four teeth.

Like elephants, people also have molar teeth. These molars are used for chewing food. But an elephant's molars are a different shape and size to human molars. And our molars are replaced only once in our lifetime. In an elephant's lifetime, its four molars are replaced five times.

back of mouth

New tooth growing out from behind old molar

Front edge of tooth has been worn away

a molar tooth

This whole section is a new tooth growing out. When the surface wears down, the ridges will show.

Ridges on tooth

Oval shape

A tooth at the front of an elephant's jaw that will eventually be replaced by the new tooth just visible at the back of the jaw.

How the teeth get replaced

As an elephant grows up, each set of four molars gets replaced by a new set of four molars. This happens five times. It happens like this: often, an elephant will put a branch into its mouth and twist the branch around with its trunk. The elephant uses the edge of its teeth to scrape and grind off the bark. So the front edge of the molars gets slowly worn away, or breaks off.

The new molars come up at the back of the elephant's mouth, and push the old molars forward and out of their way.

Every new molar grows bigger than the old one that was worn away. This is because, as the elephant grows bigger, it needs larger teeth. After five sets of molars have been worn away, from the age of about 40, the elephant grows its last, sixth set of four molars. When these last molars get worn away, the elephant has no more teeth and cannot chew its food any more. It will slowly starve, and then die. Usually this happens by the time the elephant is 60 years old.

An elephant's huge head is not made of solid bone – the skull bones have holes in them, that look like a honeycomb. Because of these holes, the skull is not too heavy, and the elephant can easily move its head around.

Elephant graveyards

A graveyard or cemetery is a place where dead people are buried. Many people believe that elephants die in their own special elephant graveyards. Elephants do not actually have graveyards, but sometimes many elephants go to the same place to die. There is a reason for this.

When elephants are old and all their teeth have worn out, they can stay alive only by eating food that is soft. Old elephants spend much of their time near water, because their food is usually softer there. When elephants can no longer chew their food, they **survive** by drinking water until they die. A few old elephants may die at the same waterhole, especially if it is the only waterhole in the area. The elephant bones that remain, close to the waterhole, make the area look like an elephant graveyard.

What is grieving?

When a person dies, that person's family is usually very sad. We say that the family is grieving. Animals do not usually grieve, but elephants are different. Elephants grieve when one of the herd dies. They show that they are grieving by picking up the dead elephant's tusks, skull and bones. They carry the bones and tusks around with them for a while. Sometimes, elephants just stand beside the dead elephant and smell it. They also gently touch the elephant's body with their trunks.

A baby elephant getting ready to drink milk from its mother's teats, which are between her front legs. The baby drinks with its mouth.

Male and female elephants

A male elephant is called a bull, and a female elephant is called a cow. It is difficult to tell the difference between the two. You have to look carefully.

Older bulls are extremely large, and much bigger than cows. Old bulls usually live alone, but sometimes they live with one or two other bulls. Cows always live in herds.

To tell the difference between a young bull and a cow, you have to look at the elephant's forehead from the side. Young bulls have round foreheads, while cows have angular foreheads. Bulls' backs are also straighter than cows' backs, which are rounded.

Bulls' testicles are hidden inside their bodies, but they have large penises – sometimes the penis is so long that it touches the ground. A cow has two big teats that hang between her front legs. Her baby drinks milk from these teats.

An elephant bull's rounded forehead.

An elephant cow's angular forehead.

Elephants have small eyes and do not see very well.

Senses

Like people, animals have five senses. The five senses are sight, smell, touch, taste and hearing. Some of an elephant's senses are very good, while others are not.

Elephants have small eyes, about the same size as a human's eyes. Because elephants have such small eyes, they do not see well. Elephants can see clearly only if an object is 50 metres in front of them or closer.

Elephants have large ears, and so they hear well. Their sense of smell is also excellent. By holding their trunks at different heights, they can smell what is around them. Elephants lift their trunks to smell the air when they think that there is danger nearby.

An elephant's sixth sense

Elephants also have a sixth sense. Like many other animals, inside their mouth, on the roof of the mouth, is a small opening. Elephants collect air in their trunks and send the air to the opening. Chemicals in the air tell them certain things. For example, an elephant can recognise another elephant by these chemicals.

Elephants have a good sense of smell.

Elephants can hear well.

Elephants use their feet to break up branches while eating.

Big feet

Elephants have very big, round feet. The front feet are rounder than the back feet, which are oval in shape. The front feet are also larger than the back feet, because they have to carry and support the elephant's head, trunk and tusks, which are very heavy.

The skin on the bottom of an elephant's feet is rough and cracked, so an elephant's **footprints** have lines in them. These lines are like a person's fingerprints – they are different in every elephant. Elephants have five toenails on their front feet, and four toenails on their back feet. As they walk, their toenails push the sand forward, leaving a small hole at the front of their footprints. This hole shows us the direction in which the elephant was walking.

The elephant uses its toenails when it is eating. First, it grasps, or holds, a tuft of grass in its trunk. Then it uses its toenails to cut the grass off at the roots. By leaving the roots in the ground, the elephant does not have to eat a mouthful of soil.

Elephants also use their feet to push fruit or short grass into a pile. They scoop this food up with their trunks.

The cracks on the soles of an elephant's foot.

An elephant's footprint, showing the cracks in its skin.

Even though elephants are enormous, they can walk silently.

Walking quietly

Elephants walk extremely quietly. If you could see the bones through the skin of an elephant's foot, you would see that the elephant is walking on its toes. Under the heel of an elephant's foot there is a big, spongy pad that is like a cushion. This soft pad spreads out when the elephant's foot touches the ground. As the elephant lifts its foot, the spongy pad shrinks again. With every step that the elephant takes, the pad takes the weight of the elephant. The pad also makes the elephant's steps very quiet.

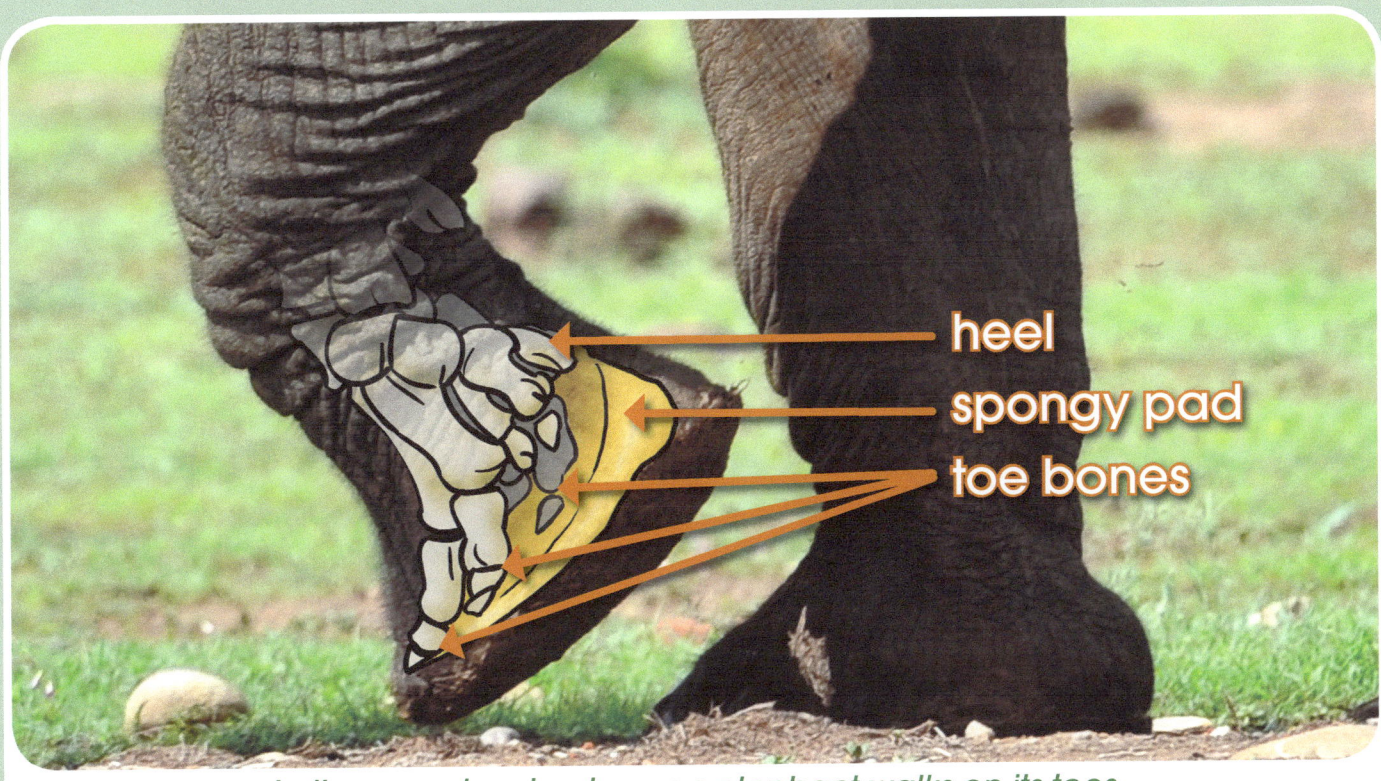

A diagram showing how an elephant walks on its toes.

When elephants travel, they stay together by communicating with low rumbling sounds.

Rumbles

Elephants talk to each other, or communicate, in different ways. They make trumpeting noises through their trunks. They scream if they are angry or excited. The way an elephant stands also sends a message. For example, an elephant that stands with its head up and its ears sticking out is angry or feels threatened, and it may charge.

But most of the time, elephants communicate by rumbling. Rumbles are soft noises that sound like the noises your tummy makes when it rumbles. But these rumbles do not come from the elephant's stomach. We call them **infrasonic** rumbles, because most of them are too deep and low for humans to hear them – only elephants can hear them. These rumbling sounds can be heard by elephants that are up to 12 kilometres away!

The rumbling sounds help elephants to stay together as a herd. When they cannot see each other in thick bush while they are feeding, they make infrasonic rumbles to tell the herd where they are. Some animal experts think that elephants pick up infrasonic sound through their feet.

An elephant flapping its ears to tell other elephants that it is excited or angry.

Elephants drink by sucking water into their trunks, and then squirting it into their mouths.

Water

Elephants need to drink water every day, and they will walk a long way to find it. If there is only a little water, for example during a drought, elephants usually chase other animals away from a waterhole. They chase away zebra, warthog and buffalo so that they have more water for themselves.

Elephants need water to help them digest and break down their food. Every day, elephants eat lots of plants, including the hard bark and roots of trees. So they need to drink between 100 and 150 litres of water a day. Sometimes, they drink all this water at one time.

Elephants are fussy drinkers and like to drink clean water. They do not like to drink muddy or dirty water from a waterhole. To make the water cleaner, an elephant will dig a hole next to the muddy waterhole. The water from the large waterhole **filters** through the sand and runs into the smaller hole. The elephant then drinks the cleaner water in the smaller hole.

Elephants can smell water that is underground. They often dig holes in dry riverbeds, so that the underground water filters into the holes. After the elephants have finished drinking from the pools that have formed, other animals come to drink. In this way, elephants help other animals to get water during dry periods.

Top left and right: Elephants really enjoy swimming! Bottom left: A young elephant climbs out of a waterhole after a swim. Bottom right: While swimming, one elephant may mount another, climbing on the other elephant's back just for fun.

Swimming

Elephants love to swim. They walk into the water until their bodies are completely covered. Then they raise their trunks above the water and use them to breathe.

Elephants spray themselves with water that they have sucked up into their trunks. They squirt water over their bodies as if they were having a shower.

Elephants have thick, tough skin. It can be up to four centimetres thick in places. Unlike other animals, elephants do not have sweat glands in their skin to help them cool down. So bathing helps elephants to cool their large bodies on hot days.

Young bulls are playful when they swim. They enjoy the water, and play-fight with each other. They push each other with the front of their bodies, and tussle or play-fight with their tusks. One elephant may climb on another elephant's back from behind. We call this mounting. When one bull elephant mounts another in the water, this is a friendly way of showing that he is stronger and more important than the other bull.

A cow elephant sprays mud over her calf to keep it cool.

Mud!

When animals lie or roll around in mud, we say that they are wallowing. Mud-wallowing is another way in which elephants keep themselves cool.

On sunny days, an elephant's back gets very hot. So the elephant uses its trunk to suck up mud, which it sprays onto its back. The layer of mud traps the dampness or wetness close to the elephant's skin. The mud also protects the skin from becoming sunburnt.

An elephant rubbing its belly on a termite mound.

If there is no mud, the elephant uses sand or dust to cover its back. It also sprays mud behind its ears, to help it cool off.

When the mud dries, the elephant's skin becomes itchy. The elephant gets rid of the mud by rubbing its body against hard objects such as rocks and tree trunks. At the same time, the elephant also rubs off ticks that are trapped in the mud. Ticks are parasites that suck the elephant's blood and can make the elephant sick.

By wallowing in mud, elephants also help the bush. The elephant's body makes a hollow, or pan, in the ground, which fills up with water when it rains. Other animals drink from these pans.

A breeding herd has elephants of all ages.

Family life

Elephants live in herds. Herds include grandmothers, mothers, daughters, sisters, aunts and cousins. The only males in the herd are babies and males that are younger than 12 years. We call this type of herd a breeding herd. The oldest cow is in charge of the herd, and she is called the matriarch.

A small herd of female and baby elephants.

Elephants live for a long time. They learn by experience, finding out what is good and what is bad for them. The older an elephant gets, the more experience it has, and the more it knows. The matriarch is the oldest in the herd, so she is the wisest. This is why she is the leader.

Because the matriarch has the most experience, she shows the herd where to find food and water. When there is a drought, elephants have to migrate, or travel far to find food and water. The matriarch remembers the different migratory routes or paths that they have taken. She leads her herd along these routes, showing them the paths that she learnt about from her great-grandmother. These paths lead to areas where there is food and water.

Elephant bulls, like these, live alone or in small groups.

Young bulls and old bulls

Bulls usually live alone. But sometimes they live together with other bulls in small groups, which we call bachelor herds.

When bulls are 12 to 14 years old, they leave the breeding herds. These bulls are still young and they have a lot to learn. So they join up with older bulls and learn from them how to behave as adults.

When younger bulls live with older bulls, we call these younger bulls *askari*. *Askari* is the Swahili word for "soldier". Swahili is a language spoken in East Africa. The name is given to the young bulls because they look as if they are bodyguards protecting the older elephants.

Bull elephants enjoy head-butting and play-fighting. They push each other with their heads, and they lock tusks. By play-fighting, the elephants find out which bull is stronger. A weaker elephant always gives in, or surrenders, to a stronger elephant. We say that the stronger elephant is **dominant**. Because the elephants play-fight to find out which bull is stronger, later they will not need to have real fights. In this way they stay away from fighting, and avoid getting hurt.

When an elephant herd gets too big, some elephants break away to form their own herd.

Clans and home ranges

If an elephant herd becomes too large, it splits up and separates into another herd. A group of closely related cows, for example a grandmother, a mother and all her calves of various ages, often breaks away and starts a new herd.

These new, smaller herds still meet up with each other. So the different herds of elephants in every area are all part of the same big family. Each big family is called a clan.

The area where a herd lives is a home range. The elephants find food and water in their home range, and bull elephants come to visit. The bull elephants in the same home range recognise each other. These bulls know which elephant is dominant, from play-fighting together when they were younger.

A cow carefully watches over her calf.

Social life

Elephants care about their family, and so we say that they are **social** animals. There are strict rules that each elephant in the herd must obey. Elephants are large animals and they could hurt each other if they did not obey these rules.

In each herd, all the elephants learn the important job of protecting and teaching the calves. A female elephant is pregnant for 22 months, which is almost two years. The time that a female is pregnant is the gestation period. The herd protects each new calf because a cow cannot have another calf for at least four years after she has given birth. Each calf is precious, and the herd does everything it can to help the calf grow up into an adult.

For the first two years of its life, an elephant calf stays close to its mother. Because elephants live for such a long time, they have a long childhood. Calves continue to learn as they grow. All the female elephants in the herd act as nannies, looking after the calves. They show the calves how to climb over things that get in the way, such as rocks or holes, and they teach them what to eat. The nannies teach and protect the calves, just as the mother does. From quite a young age, female elephants help to look after the younger elephants. In this way the females learn how to become good mothers.

What are the boys up to?

While young female elephants practise taking care of the calves, young bulls practise head-butting and play-mounting each other. These are skills that the bulls will need when they leave the herd. These skills will help to decide which bull is dominant.

This elephant is in musth. You can see this from the wet marks on the side of his forehead and on the inside of his back legs.

Musth

Elephant bulls leave the herd when they are about 12 years old. They start to mate when they are 25 to 35 years old. Before a bull can mate with a cow, he must be in musth (MUST).

When a bull is in musth, strong-smelling urine, or liquid waste, dribbles from his penis. The insides of his back legs become wet and dark green in colour, because of the urine. Liquid from glands on the sides of his head also runs down his face.

A bull that is in musth has a lot of testosterone, which is a male **hormone** that tends to make the bull aggressive and angry. The musth bull walks with a swagger – as if he is better than other bulls. He travels long distances to find a cow that he is not related to, because if he mated with a cow that he was related to, the calves would be born weak or sickly. While the musth bull is looking for cows, he makes infrasonic musth calls, to call all the cows that are ready to mate.

Young bulls are in musth for just a few days or a week at a time. Older bulls may be in musth for months at a time.

Dark marks on an elephant's face

Both bull and cow elephants have glands, called temporal glands, on the sides of their foreheads. These glands give off a smell. A wet liquid sometimes also comes from these glands and makes dark marks on the elephants' faces. When bulls are in musth, looking for females to mate with, a lot of liquid from these glands runs down their cheeks. And when cows and young elephants are afraid, liquid from the same glands also runs down their cheeks. Elephants use the tips of their trunks to smell each other's temporal glands when they greet each other.

Bulls of the same size fight each other so that the dominant bull can mate with an oestrus cow.

Finding a mate

When an elephant cow is ready to mate, we say that she is in **oestrus** or in heat. If a musth bull is looking for an oestrus cow and meets another bull along the way, the bulls will challenge each other. Younger bulls give in to older bulls and do not fight them, because older bulls are bigger and stronger. So younger bulls come out of musth when they meet big bulls. But if two bulls are the same size, they will fight, and they may even kill each other.

Bulls fight head to head, clashing their heads and tusks. They also try to stab each other's throats with their tusks. The winner mates with the oestrus cow.

Did you know?

Female elephants mate and have babies from the age of eight years. Only the biggest bulls mate with the cows, and so there is often a huge difference between the weight of the male and the female. A young oestrus cow weighs about one ton, or a bit more, while the mature musth bull weighs five to six tons. This can be quite stressful for the young cow.

Food in the poo

A bull elephant may pass up to 155 kilograms of dung in a day! But this dung is not all wasted. Dung beetles eat elephant dung. Some dung beetles roll the dung into balls. They lay their eggs in these balls and bury the balls under soil. Baboons and birds break open the dung to look for seeds and fruit to eat. Some seeds, such as marula seeds, grow well after they have passed through the stomach of an elephant. These seeds germinate, or begin to grow, after they are dropped in a pile of elephant dung.

Many dung beetles can use the same pile of elephant dung.

Food

Elephants are herbivores – they eat plants. They have to eat a huge amount every day to feed their large bodies. For this reason, elephants eat many types of plants, and different parts of a plant. An elephant's diet includes grass, herbs, water plants, bulbs, tubers, roots, fruit, flowers, bark, pods, seeds, leaves and branches.

An adult bull eats about 300 kilograms of food each day, which is about five per cent of what the bull weighs. A female eats about half this amount, or between 150 and 200 kilograms, per day. Elephants feed all day long. They even feed at night, to make sure that they eat enough food.

The elephant's food goes into its stomach, where it is digested, or broken up so that it can be used by the body. The food that is not digested passes out of the body as solid waste matter or **dung**.

Less than half of what the elephant eats is digested. The elephant's digestive system does not waste time trying to digest food that needs a lot of effort to break down. Instead, it passes the food out to make room for more food.

Eating soil

Like all animals, elephants need minerals and salts to keep their bones strong. But they do not always get enough minerals or salts from the plants that they eat. Soil is rich in minerals, so elephants sometimes chew soil. We call this geophagia (jee-oh-FAY-jee-a). Elephants use their toenails to break up soil, which they scoop into their mouths with their trunks.

An elephant sleeping with its head resting against a tree trunk.

Habits

Habits are things that animals and people do over and over again.

Elephants follow a fairly regular daily routine: they rest during the hottest part of the day, usually after they have drunk water or had a mud bath. The whole herd has the habit of resting together in the shade. When it gets cooler, the elephants continue to feed. They may have a second rest at midnight.

Elephants sleep during their resting periods. Large elephants have the habit of sleeping standing up, or leaning against a tree. Smaller elephants usually lie down on their sides to sleep.

After resting at midnight, the herd begins to feed again during the early hours of the morning. They feed until they reach a waterhole. There, they again drink and rest during the hottest time of the day.

Members of the herd protect a baby elephant from predators by walking next to it.

When danger comes

When elephants feed, they spread out over a large area and make a lot of noise while they eat. But if there is danger nearby, the whole herd suddenly goes quiet, keeping still and listening. Elephants use their trunks to smell the air. If they are afraid of what they can smell, they move away quietly. Elephants are large animals, but they can disappear quickly and silently into the bush. At times like these, elephants use infrasonic rumbles to warn one another quietly and escape without being noticed.

At other times, if the danger is out in the open, elephants may trumpet or scream loudly, to chase away the threat. The young elephants move to the middle of the herd, while the largest elephants stand on the side closest to the danger. Their big bodies form a wall that protects their young. Sometimes cows charge at lions or other enemies to chase them away.

A young calf usually travels under its mother's belly, between her legs. The calf is safe, and it also stays cool and is protected from the sun. While they are walking, the mother helps the calf to climb over things that are in the way. A young calf always stays close to its mother or to another adult elephant, and it never goes further than two metres away.

Smaller elephants eating from a tree that a big elephant has pushed over.

Helping the bush

Elephants push trees over so that they can eat the green leaves on the top of the tree. This often kills the trees. Elephants also pull bark off trees to eat the inner bark, which has water and sugars in it. The bark of a tree carries water and nutrients from its roots to the leaves. Water and nutrients make the tree grow and keep the leaves healthy. So if elephants remove all the bark around one part of the tree trunk, the tree dies.

An elephant bull uses his trunk to break off a branch.

Killing trees seems wasteful, but it actually helps the bush. By pushing trees over, elephants help smaller animals. Animals such as small antelope can eat the leaves of trees that are lying on the ground. And animals such as rodents, reptiles and birds live in fallen trees. Grass grows between the branches, and small animals make their homes in these branches. By living in the tangle of branches and soft grass, these animals are safe from predators. Sometimes, when elephants are feeding, fruit falls onto the ground and smaller animals eat this fruit.

When trees die, they fall apart and begin to rot. The nutrients from the trees go back into the soil and **fertilise** it, keeping the soil healthy so that other plants can grow.

Elephants also help to keep the bush from becoming too dense, or thick, making it easier for other animals to move around, and allowing the grass to grow. If there were no elephants, the bush would become very dense.

Elephants need big areas in which to live.

Elephants and people

In 1900, about ten million elephants lived in Africa. By 1989 there were less than 500 000 elephants living in Africa. The main reason for this is some humans' greed for ivory. Hunters shot many thousands of elephants for their tusks. People made things from the ivory, such as jewellery and piano keys.

Over the years, people moved into areas where elephants lived, planting crops on farms, and building towns and cities. Because the elephants were in the way, they were killed. This still happens, and nowadays elephants are also killed for their meat.

Elephants are large animals and they live in large herds. So they need big areas in which to live. There are cities and farms on so much of the land that nowadays there are not many wild bush areas left for elephants to live in.

Hundreds of elephant tusks that were taken away from poachers in East African countries such as Tanzania and Uganda. These tusks were being guarded in nearby Kenya until they could be destroyed.

Conservation

Conservation means protecting wildlife and the places where these animals live.

Because there are only about 400 000 to 600 000 elephants alive today, we say that elephants are **vulnerable**. If we do not protect them, they may become extinct. An animal is extinct when there are no longer any of these animals living.

In 1989, the countries that are part of CITES, which is the **Convention** on International Trade in Endangered Species, voted to put elephants on a list called Appendix 1. This means that people may no longer trade, or buy and sell, ivory.

Nowadays, the number of elephants in southern Africa is growing, because elephants are protected in game reserves. But there is still much poaching and illegal shooting of elephants in countries in East, West and Central Africa.

The bodies of elephants that were culled in a game reserve.

Culling

Elephants are protected in game reserves, and usually live in peace there. But even game reserves are not always big enough for many herds of elephant to live in – there might not be enough water and food for them all. Elephants used to be able to move around wherever they liked to find food and water. But if they cannot leave the reserve to search for food and water somewhere else, they sometimes cause a lot of damage to the trees that grow there. This may be bad for the elephants and also for other animals that live in the trees, or need the trees for food.

Some scientists say that we should cull, or kill, elephants when there are too many of them in a game reserve. But this is extremely stressful for the elephants, for two reasons. First, elephants can communicate with other herds that are far away and a herd that is being killed will let the other herds know. Second, if only some members of a herd are culled, the ones left alive will be in shock because other members of the herd are dead.

Other scientists say that game reserves should be made bigger. But if this was done, farmers would lose some of their farmland. Scientists and animal experts are therefore looking for other ways to solve the problem of controlling the number of elephants in a game reserve.

An elephant gently pushes her calf from behind as they wade through water.

Glossary

convention – a large meeting of people who have the same purpose or goal

dominant – stronger and more important

dung – an animal's solid waste matter

fertilise – to add nutrients, so that plants will grow

filters – removes dirt and impurities

footprints – marks left on the ground by feet

hormone – a substance in an animal or person's body that controls other cells in the body; sex hormones can influence the behaviour or mood of a person or animal

infrasonic – sound waves that are too deep and low to be heard by a human

matriarch – a female head of a family, herd or clan

oestrus – the times when a female animal is ready to mate

predators – animals that hunt and kill other animals for food

shrinks – makes smaller

social – spending time together as a family and as a herd

survive – to stay alive

unique – different from all others

vulnerable – animals that are in danger of becoming extinct, or dying out, in time

www.ingramcontent.com/pod-product-compliance
Lightning Source LLC
Chambersburg PA
CBHW041322290426

44108CB00004B/103